KATE SPADE

BOLD & BRIGHT HANDBAG DESIGNER

Rebecca Felix

Checkerboard
Library

An Imprint of Abdo Publishing
abdobooks.com

abdobooks.com

Published by Abdo Publishing, a division of ABDO, PO Box 398166, Minneapolis, Minnesota 55439.

Printed in the United States of America, North Mankato, Minnesota
052019
092019

Design: Aruna Rangarajan, Mighty Media, Inc.
Production: Mighty Media, Inc.
Editor: Rachael L. Thomas
Design Elements: Shutterstock Images
Cover Photograph: Getty Images
Interior Photographs: AP Images, pp. 5, 13, 21, 28 (bottom right); Getty Images, pp. 15, 23; Shutterstock Images, pp. 11, 16, 19, 25, 28 (left, middle, top right), 29 (left, right); Sonia Moskowitz/Alamy, p. 9; Wikimedia Commons, pp. 7, 27

Library of Congress Control Number: 2018966472

Publisher's Cataloging-in-Publication Data

Names: Felix, Rebecca, author.
Title: Kate Spade: bold & bright handbag designer / by Rebecca Felix
Other title: Bold & bright handbag designer
Description: Minneapolis, Minnesota : Abdo Publishing, 2020 | Series: Fashion figures | Includes online resources and index.
Identifiers: ISBN 9781532119552 (lib. bdg.) | ISBN 9781532174018 (ebook)
Subjects: LCSH: Spade, Kate (Katherine Valentine Brosnahan)--Juvenile literature. | Fashion designers--United States--Biography--Juvenile literature. | Handbags--Juvenile literature. | Women **entrepreneurs--Biography--Juvenile literature.**
Classification: DDC 746.920922 [B]--dc23

CONTENTS

CLASSIC & COLORFUL ICON

Kate Spade was a talented designer whose style had a great **impact** on American fashion in the early 2000s. Her bright, bold designs earned fans around the world and across several generations. Today, Spade's name is forever linked with her much-loved fashion label, Kate Spade New York.

Spade and her husband started Kate Spade New York in the 1990s. The brand's first items were boxy handbags in bright **hues**. From there, the label expanded to include shoes, clothing, and more. Kate Spade became a lifestyle marked by an upbeat and timeless style.

Spade's brand came to represent a chic, New York City style. But big-city fashion was not a part of Spade's upbringing. As a kid, she wasn't aware of the high-end fashion world of which she would one day become a celebrated leader.

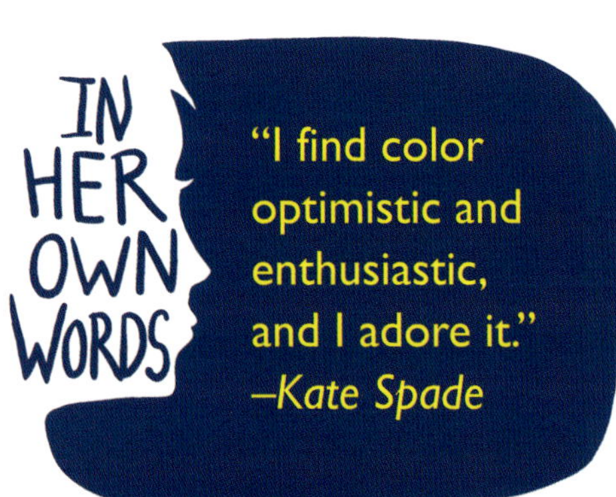

Today, colorful Kate Spade accessories are sold on every continent, in more than 400 stores!

KANSAS CITY KATE

Katherine Noel Brosnahan was born on December 24, 1962. She grew up in Kansas City, Missouri, and went by Katy or Kate. Kate was the second youngest of six children. Her mother was named June and her father Earl. Earl owned a construction business. June worked for a time as a flight attendant.

Though young Kate wasn't especially interested in fashion, her mother's style appealed to her. Kate particularly admired June's flight attendant uniform. This included boxy handbags and shoes with sharp, **clean lines**. As part of the look, June wore her hair swept up in a tidy updo. June's style influenced Kate's taste in fashion for the rest of her life.

> **FASHION FACT**
>
> Kate Spade New York briefly designed airline uniforms in 2004.

Kate attended St. Teresa's Academy, a Catholic school for girls. After graduation in 1981, Kate enrolled at Kansas State

St. Teresa's Academy is the oldest school in Kansas City.

University. Two years after that, she moved to study at Arizona State University in Tempe. It was in this sunny state where a new friendship would change her entire future.

ANDY & ARIZONA

Brosnahan studied journalism at Arizona State University for two years. During this time, she found a job in the women's department of a clothing store. There, she met Andy Spade. Andy worked in the men's department of the same store. The pair soon became friends and then began dating.

Brosnahan graduated from Arizona State University in 1985. She decided to tour Europe while Andy finished his studies. On her way back from Europe, Brosnahan's flight landed in New York.

Brosnahan didn't have enough money to buy another plane ticket. So, she decided to get a job in New York and save up money. Then, she could fly back to Arizona and be with Andy.

Brosnahan turned to a **temp agency** to find work. The agency assigned her to *Mademoiselle* magazine, where she began work as an assistant in the fashion department in 1986. This random job assignment would have a major **impact** on Brosnahan's future.

Andy and Kate Spade were life and business partners for more than 30 years.

ACCESSORIES ACE

As Brosnahan settled in at *Mademoiselle*, she planned her return to Arizona. At first, she wanted to work at the magazine for three months. Then she extended her time at the magazine to six months.

Eventually, Brosnahan realized she loved her job, and New York City too. When the magazine offered her a permanent position, Brosnahan decided to stay. Andy moved to New York to be with her.

Brosnahan's career at *Mademoiselle* flourished. By 1989, she was promoted to associate editor and put in charge of **accessories**. Two years later, she became senior fashion editor.

Though Brosnahan was successful at the magazine, she wanted a new career challenge. One night, she discussed this feeling with Andy. Andy knew of Brosnahan's **expertise** in accessories. Brosnahan collected handbags for photo shoots at *Mademoiselle,* and Andy thought she had a talent for it. He believed Brosnahan knew more about handbags than anyone.

New York City is known to be a fashion hub. Each year, New York Fashion Week attracts almost 250,000 people to the city.

Brosnahan felt that the handbag market lacked stylish yet practical bags. So, Andy suggested she create her own. Brosnahan had no background in design, so she wasn't sure where she would begin. But in the end, she decided to go for it! In 1991, Kate left *Mademoiselle* to begin designing her own fashion line.

PAPER PLANS

Brosnahan was excited to design a fashion line. At the time, she thought handbags on the market were too **complicated**. Brosnahan wanted to create handbags that were, in her words, "clean and simple and modern."

Brosnahan began by buying large sheets of paper. From those, she cut out smaller pieces and taped them together into handbag shapes. Over the next year, Brosnahan found a pattern maker to help her create patterns. The two practiced making sample bags out of any fabric they could find.

IN HER OWN WORDS

"We didn't come from fashion, so we were making it up as we went."
—Spade on her and Andy starting Kate Spade New York

Finally, Brosnahan was ready to make sample bags from the sturdy fabrics she wanted to use. But finding fabric turned out to be a challenge. Established fabric companies sold their products in very large quantities. Brosnahan wanted to start small, making only a few **prototypes**. So, she had to think about other options.

Brosnahan wondered if burlap might work. Burlap is a cheap, heavyweight fabric used to package and transport food. Brosnahan found a potato sack company that agreed to sell her a small amount of burlap. By January 1993, Brosnahan had made several prototypes of her handbag designs.

Kate Spade New York's motto is "Live Colorfully."

KATE + SPADE

Brosnahan's first **prototypes** were made of burlap. She refined the bags using nylon in bright colors and black. At last, she felt ready to **debut** her designs. But first, Brosnahan needed a brand name.

As Brosnahan thought of brand name ideas, Andy suggested Kate Spade. Andy was very involved in the development of Brosnahan's handbags. He provided support and funds. He wanted to use both their names because he and Brosnahan were partners. Brosnahan decided to go with his suggestion. The brand's official name became Kate Spade New York.

The next step in launching Kate Spade New York was showing the handbags at fashion trade shows. Trade shows are gatherings where fashion brands and designers show off their creations. Representatives from department stores visit these shows and choose items and brands they want to sell in their stores.

Anna Wintour, chief editor of *Vogue* magazine, said of Kate Spade, "There was a moment when you couldn't walk a block in New York without seeing one of her bags, which were just like her: colorful and unpretentious."

The New York Javits Center is the busiest convention center in the US. More than 40,000 companies host or attend events there each year.

In January 1993, Brosnahan and Andy **debuted** six handbag styles at a trade show at New York's Javits Center. By the end of the show, Brosnahan's handbags caught the attention of buyers from two high-end department stores, Barney's and Fred Segal.

At first, Brosnahan was upset. She had hoped for more buyers. She and Andy had already put $4,000 into the Kate Spade brand. Brosnahan was concerned about spending even more money in case the bags did not attract more buyers.

But Andy was encouraged by their start. He pushed to keep his and Brosnahan's new brand going. And his instinct turned out to be right! Three months after Kate Spade New York's **debut**, famous fashion magazine *Vogue* featured the handbags. Other fashion magazines soon did too. Celebrities began carrying Kate Spade bags.

FASHION FACT

The night before her first bags debuted, Spade decided they weren't quite right. She stayed up all night removing the brand label from the inside of each bag and hand-sewing it to the outside.

Brosnahan believed her bags were popular because they were different from what other fashion brands were making. The more people saw Brosnahan's **innovative** designs, the more interest and demand for Kate Spade items grew.

SIMPLE, SLEEK SENSATIONS

People saw something special in Kate Spade New York. As the company **debuted** more handbags, Brosnahan's designs became known for their classic shapes and bright colors. Brosnahan's taste was called elegant and fun, **preppy** yet **unique**.

Brosnahan's **philosophy** was to keep things simple. One of Kate Spade's most popular early designs was the Sam bag. The Sam was a boxy, practical bag of black nylon. Buyers loved its shape. The Sam soon became a **fashion statement** for trendy New Yorkers.

In 1993, Brosnahan and Andy rented a loft in Tribeca, New York. It served as their home and office. The following year, Kate and Andy married at this location. Brosnahan's name now matched her brand. She became Kate Spade.

By 1995, Kate Spade New York was booming. Its sales had soared from $100,000 in 1993 to $1.5 million! Department stores Saks Fifth Avenue and Neiman Marcus ordered more than 20,000 Kate Spade bags that year. Spade's designs were in demand across the country.

Early Kate Spade New York handbags were priced between $100 and $400. These prices were less than those of other designer handbags at the time, which often sold for thousands of dollars.

FIRST STORE & FASHION AWARDS

Demand for Kate Spade products soon outgrew the Spades' Tribeca loft space. So in 1996, they opened a small shop in Manhattan to sell Kate Spade handbags. It was a great success! The store had $6 million in sales its first year.

The same year, the Council of Fashion Designers of America (CFDA) officially recognized Spade's talents. The organization gave Spade the America's New Fashion Talent in **Accessories** award. Two years later, the CFDA named her Best Accessory Designer.

By 1998, Kate Spade New York had opened new stores in Boston, Massachusetts, Los Angeles, California, and Tokyo, Japan. The following year, the Spades sold 56 percent of their business to the Neiman Marcus Group for $33.6 million.

FASHION FACT

Recognition from the CFDA is considered one of the highest honors in the fashion industry.

Spade and her brother-in-law, actor David Spade, attend a CFDA award ceremony.

PUBLISHING, PARTNERS & PARENTHOOD

Kate Spade New York continued to evolve and expand. The brand soon offered clothing, shoes, home decor, eyewear, and more. In 2000, Spade also published a book called *Contents*. The book examines the items people keep and carry within their handbags.

In 2002, *Glamour* magazine named Spade Woman of the Year. Two years later, Spade published three more books titled *Manners*, *Occasions*, and *Style*. These books share Spade's **philosophies** on life, events, and design.

By this time, Kate Spade New York was worth $70 million. And as the Spades' brand continued to grow, so did their family. In February 2005, Spade and Andy had a daughter. They named her Frances Beatrix.

The Spades decided they wanted to devote more time to raising their daughter. So in 2006, the couple sold their remaining shares of Kate Spade New York to the Neiman Marcus Group for $59 million.

Kate and Andy Spade with their daughter, Frances Beatrix

Just one week later, the Neiman Marcus Group sold the brand to Liz Claiborne, Inc. for $124 million. Because the Spades no longer owned any part of Kate Spade New York, they did not receive any money from that sale.

STARTING FRESH

After Kate Spade New York was sold, Spade's main focus became raising her daughter. Spade also became involved at Frances's school and with helping other children. In 2006, she became co-chair of the board for the New York Center for Children. The organization helps children who have suffered **abuse**.

Though Spade's work for children became her passion, she remained interested in fashion. In 2016, she got back into the business. That year, the Spades launched the fashion line Frances Valentine.

Spade changed her last name to Valentine to **align** with the Frances Valentine brand. She hoped this would help separate the Valentine brand from Kate Spade New York.

FASHION FACT

By 2018, there were more than 140 Kate Spade stores in the United States and more than 175 around the world.

FRANCES VALENTINE

Frances Valentine has a classic, clean style similar to Kate Spade New York. The brand focuses mainly on shoes but also offers jewelry and handbags.

Spade liked the change that came with a new project. She was proud of the Kate Spade New York brand. But being the face of such a successful company wasn't always what Spade wanted. Frances Valentine allowed her to work more behind the scenes and concentrate on design.

FASHION LEGEND

Frances Valentine created buzz and interest in the design world. But in 2018, Spade's name returned to headlines for another reason. On June 5, Spade died at age 55. The designer took her own life.

Family, friends, and fans alike were shocked and saddened by Spade's death. To honor the designer, many people shared photos on social media of their first or favorite Kate Spade handbags. The CFDA also recognized Spade's influence, saying she had forever influenced how the world viewed American **accessories**.

IN HER OWN WORDS

"I hope that people remember me not just as a good businesswoman but as a great friend—and a heck of a lot of fun."
—*Spade, 2002 Glamour Women of the Year interview*

Though Spade is gone, her influence lives on. As designer Cynthia Rowley said, "No one had style like Kate. She lit up the room the minute she walked in and shook up the industry with her box bag and colorful life."

At the time of Kate Spade's death, the fashionista had a net worth of about $200 million.

kate spade
TIMELINE
1962
Katherine Noel Brosnahan is born on December 24, in Kansas City, Missouri.
1983
Kate attends Arizona State University, where she meets Andy Spade.
1985
Kate graduates from college, travels to Europe, and moves to New York.
1986–1991
Kate works at *Mademoiselle* magazine.
1993
Kate and Andy debut Kate Spade New York handbags.
1994
Kate marries Andy and changes her name to Kate Spade.

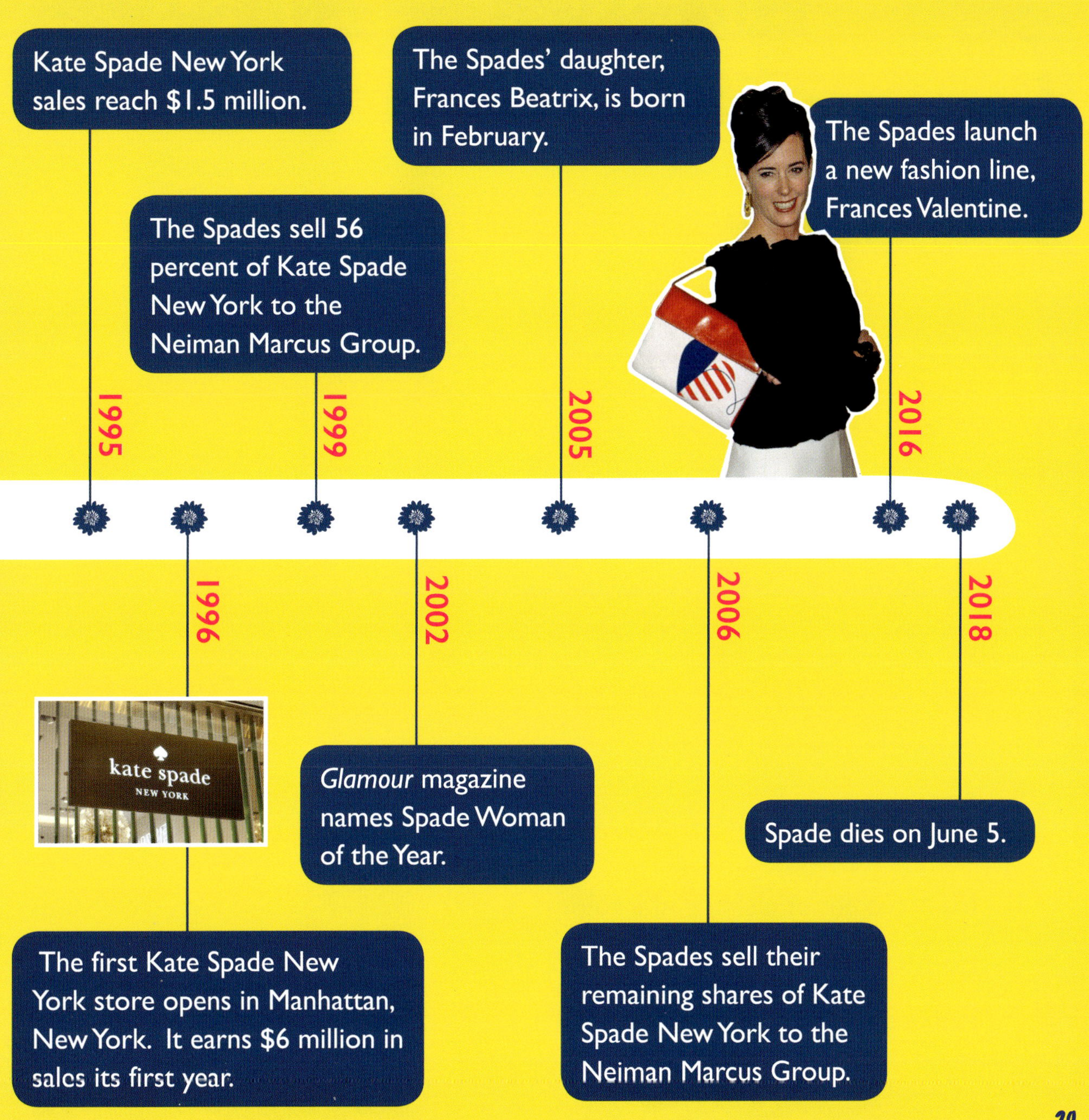
1995
Kate Spade New York sales reach $1.5 million.
1996
kate spade
NEW YORK
The first Kate Spade New York store opens in Manhattan, New York. It earns $6 million in sales its first year.
1999
The Spades sell 56 percent of Kate Spade New York to the Neiman Marcus Group.
2002
Glamour magazine names Spade Woman of the Year.
2005
The Spades' daughter, Frances Beatrix, is born in February.
2006
The Spades sell their remaining shares of Kate Spade New York to the Neiman Marcus Group.
2016
The Spades launch a new fashion line, Frances Valentine.
2018
Spade dies on June 5.

GLOSSARY

abuse—physical or verbal mistreatment of a person or object.

accessory—a small item that you wear with your clothes, such as a belt, scarf, or gloves.

align—to be in line with something. Ideas that complement each other are described as being aligned.

clean lines—appealing, well-designed lines with little disturbance or unnecessary embellishments.

complicated—having elaborately combined parts.

debut—a first appearance. To debut something is to present or perform it for the first time.

expertise—a high-level skill set.

fashion statement—a message that is communicated by a fashionable item or style.

hue—a color or a shade of a color.

impact—a strong effect on something.

innovative—marked by a new idea, method, or device.

philosophy (fuh-LAH-suh-fee)—a set of ideas about knowledge and truth.

preppy—a style of dress inspired by a classic, neat appearance.

prototype—an early model of a product on which future versions can be modeled.

temp agency—an organization that looks for temporary work on behalf of a client.

unique (yoo-NEEK)—being the only one of its kind.

ONLINE RESOURCES

To learn more about Kate Spade, please visit **abdobooklinks.com** or scan this QR code. These links are routinely monitored and updated to provide the most current information available.

INDEX